Being a

GOOD
DAD

When

You

Didn't

Have

One

TIM
WESEMANN

Beacon Hill Press of Kansas City
Kansas City, Missouri

Copyright 2002
by Beacon Hill Press of Kansas City

ISBN: 083-411-951X

Printed in the
United States of America

Cover Design: Kevin Williamson
Cover Photo: Greg Whitaker

10 9 8 7 6 5 4 3 2 1

No doubt about it . . .
for my dad.
We'll have plenty of time to catch up in heaven.

Contents

Preface

Being a good dad when you didn't have one. Hmmm—for the most part, I guess I can say that I'm a good dad. You should probably ask my three children. You should also ask my Heavenly Father. There have been marks on each end of the spectrum, I suppose. And when my marks for fatherhood are on the low end, I praise God for His graceful forgiveness and my children for the same gift. When the marks are higher, I can give glory only to the Father of all fathers—our Father who art in heaven.

Did I have a good dad growing up? I believe he would have been, but I never met him. I never heard his voice. I never played catch with him. I never attended a father-son banquet with him. Do I want to be a great dad even though I didn't have one in my life? Yes. Definitely.

I imagine the reason that most of you are holding this book in your hands is that you're in the same boat. You've been called to be a father, yet you grew up without a father in your life. While we may be in the same boat, we all came from a variety of backgrounds. That's the challenge of this book.

Acknowledgments

Thanks to Jeanette Littleton and Judi Perry and all the other staff members at Beacon Hill Press of Kansas City who had a hand in the publication of this work. Also, I thank the Mount Hermon Writers' Conference, where editor, writer, and manuscript ideas met. I greatly appreciate Linda Rogers for her editing work before the manuscript was sent. Thanks to the many prayer partners who attached themselves to this project and God's hands.

I also thank the fatherless dads who shared their stories for this book. God bless your journey through dadhood, following the lead of our Heavenly Father. And thanks, Lord, for the gift of my brothers and sister—Ted, Don, and Cathy—whose time with our dad was also cut short.

Finally, a special thanks to three loving, gifted, fun, and faith-filled children who call Chiara and me Mom and Dad—Christopher, Sarah, and Benjamin.

First and foremost, they are our fathers; and whatever magic we had with them, even if it is for just a few of our very early years, profoundly affects us for the rest of our lives.

—Cyra McFadden

I don't remember my father. And that scared me about being a father. How could I know how to be one? But I also thought that by being a father—the father I wanted—I'd finally have a father.

—Samuel
In *"Legacy,"* by Linda Spence

I grew up with an absent father. He was a physician and was so busy helping other people that he paid no attention to us. He was absent in that way. In school one day, when I was a young child, we were to draw a picture of what our father did for a living. I drew many circles on the paper. When asked about it, I said, "My father makes rounds and rounds and rounds." He was always making rounds at the hospital. That is the only time I ever spent any time with him, and it was always with others. Never any private time. I have three sons. When my wife and I divorced, my older sons took it very hard and became angry. I have an incredible relationship with my seven-year-old.

—Ken, a physician, age 61

1

Once upon a Time
The Importance of Knowing Your Story

Once upon a time there was a mother and a father and their little boy. And they all lived happily ever after.

If that's just a fairy tale to you and not the way your life really was, it may affect your relationships, job habits, decisions, and your own calling to fatherhood.

We all want a "happily ever after." But as fatherless fathers, we know life doesn't always turn out that way. It isn't much fun to read stories about divorce, parental abandonment, fathers in prison or mental institutions, or even death. We would rather focus on "happily ever after." And that's a good place for us to focus—future happiness for fatherless fathers. Even if our parents didn't get to live that happiness on earth, that doesn't mean we can't live it with our families. It's also a fact that before we move forward, we have to deal with the reality and pain of the past. Some of you have been dealing with that for years. Others of you are just beginning to open the wounds and look inside.

Our stories are all different, yet we share a common bond. We grew up without dads. But now we're fathers ourselves, and we desire to be better fathers to our children.

Jon's parents divorced when he was 5 years old. His dad moved out of state a year later. By the time he was 10, it took photographs to remind him of what his father looked like.

Darrell's mom gave birth to him on her 17th birthday. Three of her classmates could have been Darrell's father. His mom didn't know or care, and she never pursued trying to find out. For the most part, Darrell's grandmother raised him.

When T. J. was 7, his dad committed suicide. He has no memories of his father except for finding him lying in a pool of blood in the basement.

Ray's dad was in and out of prison more than he was in and out of the house. The day Ray slammed his first home run was the same day his dad was thrown into the slammer for good.

Mark's father went to work on a Monday morning and didn't come back until Tuesday evening—seven years later. By then, his mom wasn't in a welcoming mood.

Odom isn't sure who his father is. But then again, neither is his father, who suffers from multiple personalities and makes his home in a mental institution.

Marlin's parents separated when he was 3. They got back together when he was 4½. They separated again the next year. By his sixth Christmas they were divorced. His mom remarried when Marlin was 13, just in time for his rebellious teens.

Manny's dad died of a massive heart attack while jogging. Manny was only 5 at the time. His three older sisters tried to keep his dad's memory alive through stories and photos. Manny appreciates their efforts, but he realizes his dad isn't coming back.

Parker lived with his mom and dad until he left for college. His dad lived with them. Parker knew his dad was there, because he would pass him in the hall sometimes. He would sometimes hear him on the phone talking business late at night. To say the least, their relationship was not an intimate one. So it's no surprise that Parker doesn't remember his father ever crying. What's remarkable is that he doesn't remember ever hearing him laugh either. So Parker joins the group of fatherless fathers.

It doesn't take long to realize that many fathers walk into parenthood carrying some heavy baggage—emotional, mental, even spiritual. Sometimes this baggage is manifested in behavioral disorders, self-esteem issues, abuse, depression, or anger—anger at parents or even God. Our stories are all very different. I pray that the reason you're reading this is that you're anxious to receive God's hope, encouragement, and grace.

I've been told that my mother and father were very happy together. It's just that their happy life together was cut short. They didn't even get to celebrate their first wedding anniversary. One week shy of that celebration, my mother faced "till death us do part."

The marriage between my mom and my dad was her first and his second. My dad and his first wife, Libby (Elizabeth), had three children during their 12-year marriage. Then the cruelty of cancer ended Libby's life early in 1958. My father and his three young children, ages 10, 7, and 4, suddenly found themselves in a home without a mother.

All three of Orville and Libby's children attended a Christian school, and all had the same kindergarten teacher—my mom. My parents came to know each other on a personal level after Libby's death and eventually fell in love and got married. Seven months into their marriage my mom became pregnant with me.

Late in 1959 my dad was involved in an accident at the lead company where he worked in maintenance. Burned over 90 percent of his body, he spent two and a half weeks struggling in the hospital. On December 21, 1959, he died at the young age of 34. It was four days before Christmas and exactly four months before my birth.

Within 2 years, my half-brothers and half-sister lost

both their parents. With God's strength, help, and guidance, my mom raised the four of us without a husband.

Twenty-six years later, in November 1985, my mother died of bone cancer. Two days after my mother's funeral, my wife, Chiara, bought an early pregnancy test and we found out that we were expecting our first child.

What great news! My wife is expecting a baby! Then it hit me—I don't know what to expect. I don't know what it's like to be a father. I grew up without a dad, and now I'm going to have a little boy or girl calling me "Daddy" and expecting me to know how to respond. I was nervous about becoming a father. There was no permanent role model—good or bad—in my case, no father to run to when I needed answers to questions. And now that my mom had died, I couldn't even call on the one who played the dual role of mother and father during my life. I was overwhelmed.

Your Turn

What's your story? How much (and what kind of) baggage are you carrying with you into the adventure of parenting?

_____

_____

_____

_____

_____

_____

_____

_____

_____

A person's a person no matter how small.

—Theodor Geisel (Dr. Seuss)

My father abandoned me when I was 4. I felt disconnected and angry at authority for almost 40 years. I unconsciously carried a mistrust of men that kept me from fully trusting myself and relationships with other men. There were very few men I allowed to really see the man inside. Fortunately for me, one of those men was my older brother.

He saw the wounds I carried and how they were impacting my life as a father and husband. He suggested I might try attending a men's weekend. The only prerequisite was that I had to trust him, men, and the process.

I was able to fully address the grief and loss I had repressed since I was a little boy. I am now capable of being fully present in my relationship with my 18-year-old daughter because of being able to acknowledge that abandoned little boy who lived inside me.

—Tony

2

Fatherless Children Grow Up to Be Fatherless Fathers
The Importance of Knowing the Facts

When I began writing this book, I started with my experiences as a fatherless father. But then I started researching the subject, and my eyes were opened to a whole new world. I found a large group of other dads who had grown up without fathers, and they were dragging extremely heavy baggage from their childhood into their relationships with their own children.

I found staggering statistics about children who come from homes without fathers. This is when we get to look in the mirror. I warn you: sometimes what you'll see will be ugly. But it's very important that we spend the time to look —and not with just a quick glance. As you consider these statistics, remember that the fatherless children they profile grow up to be fatherless fathers. Not only are we called to the challenging role of fathering without a father, but also the baggage we bring with us into our homes needs to be dealt with as we strive to be the best fathers we can be.

I never took a class on statistics in college. I found the subject intimidating. And I'm intimidated by some of the following information, most of which comes from reports of the 1990s as the number of households operating without fathers grew in the United States, and the subject became a timely one.

With about 40 percent of children growing up without fathers, it's important to note that, in general, children deprived of close contact with their fathers are more likely to have difficulty adjusting socially, developing a positive self-image, and dealing with frustration.

The effects of fatherlessness can be seen in the area of behavioral disorders, runaways, high school dropouts, chemical abuse, suicides, and juvenile delinquency. United States data shows the following from a report of the Coalition of Parent Support:

- 85 percent of all children who exhibit behavioral disorders come from fatherless homes (Source: Centers for Disease Control).
- 90 percent of all homeless and runaway children are from fatherless homes (Source: United States Department of Health and Human Services, Bureau of the Census).
- 71 percent of all high school dropouts come from fatherless homes (Source: National Principals Association Report on the State of High Schools).
- 75 percent of all adolescent patients in chemical abuse centers come from fatherless homes (Source: *Rainbows for All God's Children*).
- 63 percent of youth who commit suicide are from fatherless homes (Source: United States Department of Health and Human Services, Bureau of the Census).
- 70 percent of juveniles in state-operated institutions come from fatherless homes (Source: United States Department of Justice, *Special Report*, September 1988).
- 80 percent of rapists motivated by displaced anger

come from fatherless homes (Source: *Criminal Justice and Behavior*, 1978, 14:403-26).

o 71 percent of teenage pregnancies are to children of single parents (Source: United States Department of Health and Human Services).

These statistics translate to mean that children from a fatherless home are

5 times more likely to commit suicide;

32 times more likely to run away;

20 times more likely to have behavioral disorders;

14 times more likely to commit rape;

9 times more likely to drop out of high school;

10 times more likely to abuse chemical substances;

9 times more likely to end up in state-operated institutions.

A 1991 report by the United States Department of Health and Human Services regarding hyperactivity within families shows that between the ages of 5 and 17, hyperactivity is found in children living with

Both biological parents   34.9%

Divorced mother and no father   58.1%

Unwed mother   38.9%

Mother and stepfather   55.1%

Similar patterns are found in other indicators of behavioral problems such as antisocial behavior, anxiety or depression, headstrong behavior, dependency (never-married mother is highest), and peer conflict or social withdrawal.

The statistics are stunning. In preparing to write this book, I considered my personal situation of growing up without a father. My eyes were opened to deeper issues as I contemplated this information regarding fathers who came from fatherless homes. There are a lot of hurting fathers out there. Maybe you're one of them.

My situation was probably a little different than many of yours. Since my father died four months before my birth, I have absolutely no memory of him. I have no pictures of him holding me. There are no videos showing him interacting with me. I don't want to take anything away from those who are dealing with the pain and grief of a father's death, but as one whose father died, I found helpful thoughts in *The Measure of a Man*, by Jerome Shapirio (1993, 101). He writes,

> One form of permanent physical separation does not seem to be as devastating as desertion, particularly to sons. This is the case when the father has died. In spite of the complete absence of their fathers, these males tend to adapt better than sons whose fathers are absent by choice. A critical factor here is that Mother may have very positive memories of her husband and will talk a lot about him to her son. This helps create a positive symbolic image of the father that partially compensates for his physical absence.

If you find yourself among the statistics in this chapter, hopefully you realize your need for help. The next step may be to seek out solid Christian counseling to help you confront the past and move into the present, looking forward to a bright future. Yes, God can work through counselors, psychiatrists, and psychologists. He may even provide you with help through medication. His desire is to help fathers become great gifts to their children, and He may do that in a variety of ways.

Finally, realize that God doesn't look at you as a statistic. He sees you with compassion, He offers forgiveness for your sins and any accompanying guilt, and He wants to show you how to become a new creation.

Your Turn

How did these statistics strike you? As you look back at your life, did you find yourself a candidate for one of the categories regarding the effects of fatherlessness? What past issues must you deal with in order to become the kind of father your Heavenly Father desires you to be to your children?

_____

_____

_____

_____

_____

_____

_____

_____

_____

_____

_____

_____

_____

_____

_____

_____

_____

_____

_____

_____

_____

My father and mother were never married. Any time that I asked about my father, I was given very vague information. At age 35 I developed some unusual medical symptoms that indicated I had either a serious disease or a genetically linked deficiency. No one was sure which. My mother finally gave me some information about my father in order to prevent me from having to undergo some invasive testing. I contacted him, and he gave me the medical information I needed, but he really did not want to have anything to do with me. The pain of rejection was devastating. At the time I was a successful businessman, and the rejection still hurt.

Interestingly enough, he stopped by my office a few months ago and wanted to ask my forgiveness for the years of neglect and rejection. He had recently suffered a stroke and felt his life was drawing to an end. I assured him that he was forgiven, but, once again, I experienced a deep sense of hurt.

I remember a number of things from my childhood and young adulthood. I remember not having a sense of identity. We gain a perspective on who we are from our parents. When one parent is missing, part of who we are is not available. I remember fantasizing about him.

I also missed a sense of security. If one parent had already abandoned me, perhaps the other one would too.

It is difficult for a single-parent child to see himself as lovable when one of the two people who is supposed to love him most isn't there.

I also felt somehow less valuable than other kids. I was very lucky in that a caring church helped me fill in some of the gaps. They gave me love. They gave me value. They cared for me. In a way, I replaced my earthly father with a Heavenly Father.

Did I carry baggage into adulthood? Of course. I didn't have a clue about how a family was supposed to work. I still work to be trusting. After all, from my perspective, one of the most important people in my life proved that he could not be trusted. I also had some problems with security for a number of years. It took a lot of work.

It was a struggle for me to get through the first 35 years of my life. I was very successful professionally and financially, but my family skills were lacking. My faith made all the difference.

—A father wishing to remain anonymous

3

Our Father at Work
The Importance of Living in the Present

The statistics we've just looked at might discourage you and cause you to think we can't be great fathers. The truth is, we may be bearing too much of the burden ourselves. That's why a look at the work our Heavenly Father has done for us is so important as we seek to develop into great fathers.

Several of my father's friends have told me that one of the things my dad loved was working on our house and acreage—building, remodeling, and creating. In fact, that's one of the strongest memories my brothers and sister have of him—continually working around our house on behalf of his family.

Our Heavenly Father worked on our behalf as well. He gave up His Son to die on a cross to pay for our sins, change our lives, and give us eternal life in heaven.

Are you starting to see the big picture? Even if you don't feel that you're carrying a lot of burdens because you grew up without a father, all of us are carrying the weight of sin in our daily lives. That's why every day we need to examine, experience, and exalt our Savior and His life-changing sacrifice on the Cross. In our time alone with Him we can travel to the outskirts of Jerusalem to witness His suffering. We can sit right at His feet—feet bloodied by nails driven through them. Through His death and resurrection, Jesus Christ offers forgiveness and victory for fatherless fathers who are failing, faltering, and even those who are faithful. And He brings these gifts not only to fathers but also to all who place their faith in Him.

It was on the Cross that Jesus Christ took upon himself the sins of the entire world. If you ever thought that the hurt you experienced from growing up without a father was some kind of punishment from God—that's not true. If you thought you were to blame for your father abandoning your family or your parents' divorce and now God was punishing you in some way—forget it. Leave those lies at the Cross. Leave the guilt at the Cross. And leave your sins at the Cross. Rejoice in the impact of God's gift of forgiveness and immerse yourself in the freeing power of grace.

One of the problems we have in accepting this gift is that Satan wants to deceive us. He plants seeds of bitterness in our hearts. He deceives us with false models of what a healthy, balanced life looks and feels like. He whittles away at our solid relationships with his tools of jealousy, inappropriate anger, spite, and vengeance. He assails us with words that hurt. Satan attempts to blast our Christian homes and dads who seek to serve our Heavenly Father.

That's why it's so important that we continually visit the Cross and the empty tomb. It's through the Cross that Jesus secured our forgiveness and imbued us with the Holy Spirit.

Fathers often feel like they need to fix everything. But earthly fathers can't create a new heart and mind focused on the Heavenly Father's ways and will. It's only God who can make us into new creations—forgiven and faithful fathers who love the Lord, our families, and others. Fatherless fathers sometimes work overtime trying to fix things within their families because they feel their family of origin needed so much mending. They don't want to raise their children in a home that's an emotional, mental, or spiritual fixer-upper. We need to realize that we can't fix everything.

One evening when I was shopping at a mall with my family, we came upon a clown who was giving away smiles to shoppers as he shaped balloons into poodles, flowers, swords, and more. Our children seemed quite impressed, even though recently, while clowning around at home, I had made my own balloon creations for them. OK—I admit that my snake and hotdog-shaped balloons left something to be desired, but I tried!

Balloon sculptures are an art form that one must appreciate quickly, because they rarely last long. Such was the case with Benjamin's balloon that evening. As soon as we got into the car, we heard a pop followed by a moment of silence. Then came the "ohhhh" sound, signaling joy was deflating from his body.

Before we could extend our sympathies, Benjamin spoke up: "Can you fix it?" Obviously, he took last night's game of "SuperParents" a bit too seriously. The class we took called "Consoling Children" failed us as we simply said, "No."

Benjamin had an idea. "But when we get home you could sew it back together!"

Some things are humanly impossible to fix. For many fathers, that's tough to accept. Some men have been struck with Tim-the-Tool-Man-itus. One of the symptoms is "I can fix anything."

Most fathers can't fix a daughter's heart that's been broken by her first love. It's next to impossible for fathers to repair the damage caused by hurtful words hurled in anger at their children. No man can actually remove from his wife's memory degrading words that were spoken in frustration. A father cannot reverse time and change his decision to work late instead of attending his child's program. No father can change the past. No father can save the soul of a family member—no earthly father, that is. No parent can fix a balloon sword with needle and thread. It's impossible.

But with God our Father nothing is impossible. Ask the aging Abraham and his hysterical wife, Sarah, about that. At their age the thought of pregnancy was inconceivable to them. Or ask Mary and Joseph about what's impossible. Ask Saul's friends if they thought he could possibly become an apostle for the Morning Star. Inquire of the rich ruler about the possibility of getting into heaven on his own.

We can't fix everything and be saviors. Jesus has done that.

All around us are other fathers whose dreams have blown up in their faces. Broken lives are everywhere, and repair seems impossible. But those who have been hurt and disappointed can lay their needs at the foot of the Cross. Our Father has overpowered and defeated Satan. Through the cross of Jesus, we'll find reconciliation for building relationships between God and man, between men and women, and between children and parents. What a promise to hold to as God builds our Christian homes!

Your Turn

What's the greatest thing God has done for you? Write your thoughts regarding what Jesus did for you on the Cross. How has His sacrifice on the Cross affected and changed your past struggles, present pain, and future plans?

_____

_____

_____

_____

_____

My father was a pastor who died when I was 3 years old. I'm the father of a wonderful 14-year-old boy who grew up quite well, sometimes in spite of me. I say that not because I think I was a rotten father, but because I had no real example of father-hood to model myself after. I think part of the reason I was a reasonably good father is because I had a marvelous mother who spared no sacrifice to bring us up as my dad would have wanted. I also had several male role models in my life who were continuously telling me how wonderful my father was. I had adult males in my life growing up, but no one who tried to take the place of my father. They always spoke of him in a very positive light, and I can never remember anyone speaking ill of him.

I do remember going through a stage in my life when I was angry with him. He died at the age of 41 from liver cancer, and I mistakenly assumed that it was due mainly to his smoking. I have since found out that his death was primarily due to a condition called hemochromatosis. I think that when I got my act together and convinced myself that he wasn't out to hurt me by dying (I was pretty young when I thought that), it made me a better father. I took what I knew of him from what my mom, my brothers and sisters, and my friends and relatives told me, added in what I knew he believed in and stood for, added what I believed and stood for, and then trusted God to provide me with the insights to do what was right and teach the right things.

I do remember dreading the annual father-son banquet at school because I had to go with my godfather, and the other guys were there with their fathers. But I think that helped me to want to be there for all my son's events. All in all, I wouldn't wish losing your father at the age of 3 on anybody. I also believe that I had a great support system in place and the love of immediate family, extended family, and spiritual family. What I try to do is duplicate that support system for my son and then be the kind of father I wanted.

—Mark

Learning from the Ultimate Father

The Importance of Our Father Who Art in Heaven

*O*ur Father which art in heaven, Hallowed be thy name . . . You've likely prayed this prayer many times, but do you really know the One to whom you're praying? He's called "Father." An intimate name. A name by which you're known. If you haven't truly gotten to know Him, you're in for a treat. He has a unique fathering style that moves not only hearts but also mountains. Credentials, you ask? Let's see—He has raised His share of children (in more ways than one). His Son, Jesus Christ, was given as a sacrifice on a cross for the forgiveness of your sins and mine, along with our eternal salvation. That's how much your Heavenly Father loves you! He created each of us and even knew us before the creation of the world.

It's also important to know that God, our Heavenly Father, cannot lie. He will never leave His children. This Father wants what's best for us and promises to take whatever we've been dealing with and work it into something beautiful for the good of those who place their lives in His hands.

Trusting Him already? Good. It's of great importance to get to know Him not only as God but also as Father—*your* Father.

Numerous fatherless fathers have shared with me their difficulties in relating to God as Father. To Jesus, God's

Son, the world's Savior? No problem. To God the Holy Spirit—the Creator and Sustainer of faith? No difficulties there. But God as Father is another story.

Your earthly father and your Heavenly Father are completely different creatures. Actually, one is the Creator and the other is the created. One is perfect. The other has flaws. Although earthly fathers are called to mirror the ways of the Heavenly Father, they fall short of perfection. Our fathers weren't the only ones to fall short. Just look in the mirror and you'll see someone else who has done the same. Thankfully we have God's forgiveness to reshape us as His new creatures.

Fathering without the experience of having a father can be intimidating. If you're feeling less than confident in this role, explore the possibilities available for your calling. You can gain confidence in your role. Let's look at some examples of God's faithfulness in providing for those in need of His leadership.

The Heavenly Father has left us a textbook to follow as we learn from Him—the Bible. Start by looking at an Old Testament story found in 1 Kings 17:1-16. Here we find Elijah, a prophet of God. The Father informed Elijah that there would be neither dew nor rain in the next few years, and Elijah then informed the king of the bleak weather forecast.

God not only knew the needs of this faithful man, but also He met those needs. He gave Elijah directions to follow, and the prophet obeyed without question. He led him to a brook of water, the Kerith Ravine, where he had water to drink. And so Elijah wouldn't have to experience ravenous hunger, the God of creation ordered ravens to bring him bread and meat in the morning and evening. The Father took care of His child, who at one point in his life struggled without something he needed.

The drought finally got the best of that brook, and it dried up. Elijah found himself without something again—food and water. But God continued to care for Elijah and guide him. The word of the Lord came to him, saying, "Go at once to Zarephath of Sidon and stay there. I have commanded a widow in that place to supply you with food" (v. 9). So Elijah went. No questions. No whining. Elijah trusted the Lord to care for His people who needed help. As you read the rest of the verses, you find that the widow had only a handful of flour and a little oil for herself and her son. Elijah said, "Don't be afraid" (v. 13). Those are great words of confidence for fatherless fathers as well as frightened widows. *Don't be afraid!* The Lord will meet your needs. In this case, the jar of flour was miraculously never used up, and the jug of oil did not run dry.

Some important points to take from this story:

- Don't doubt, even in times of drought in your journey through the land of fatherhood.
- Don't doubt the power of God to strengthen, nourish, and satisfy in what you see as a time of drought in your relationships with your children.
- Remember to be open to His wisdom and guidance.
- Be open to allowing God to use you in different ways. Maybe you feel that you're in a parenting rut—a ravine that's run dry.
- Have fun exploring new things to do with your children. Approach new subjects when talking with them.
- Instead of just spending time sitting with your child feeding crumbs to the ravens, let the Creator feed you the feast he has prepared especially for you.

This story can also teach us a simple message that's

found on a little card we have in our kitchen window. It reads, "Where God guides, He provides."

Jesus' public ministry began when He was about 30 years old (Luke 3:23). The majority of the four Gospels cover the public ministry of Jesus. And during those final years of His life, Jesus' father—His stepfather to be precise—Joseph, is not found in any of the recorded events, including this wedding feast. The last mention of Jesus' father is when He was 12 years old and His family traveled to Jerusalem for the Feast of the Passover. It seems obvious that at some point when Jesus was between 12 and 30 years of age, His father must have died. Although Scripture doesn't mention this, light is shed on the subject when Jesus speaks from the Cross, placing His mother, Mary, into the care of John. If Joseph had been alive, there would be no need for Him to do this.

I mention this because it has always been a comfort to me to know that Jesus understood what it was like for me, without a father. He invites all who have lost a father, for whatever reason, to stand under His understanding of the situation.

In John 2 we find Jesus, His mother, and the disciples at a wedding feast. In those days, wedding celebrations usually lasted a week. Everything was going smoothly until they ran completely out of wine. At first glance this may not sound like a major problem, but in those days the offense was grounds for a lawsuit.

It was Jesus' mother who informed Him of the problem. She told the servants, "Do whatever he tells you" (v. 5). The servants obeyed when Jesus instructed them to fill with water the six stone jars that were nearby. Each of these jars held between 20 to 30 gallons. The account in

John's Gospel immediately tells us that they filled them to the brim (v. 7). The jars probably weighed about 100 pounds each. Now add 20 to 30 gallons of water, and you add 200 or 250 pounds. Remember also that they didn't have running water. The servants probably had to go to the town well and carry back buckets to fill the jars, maybe a couple of gallons at a time. What a task! Yet they persevered, and the six jars were eventually filled to the brim. Following Jesus' command, the servants took some of the water, which Jesus turned to wine, to the master of the banquet. He tasted it and referred to it as "the best."

As dads *without* dads, there are so many lessons to learn here. We're reminded again, as in Elijah's story, to trust and follow God's guidance. Mary told the servants, "Do whatever he tells you." Why should they listen to this little Jewish woman? They listened not only to her but also to her Son, Jesus. And what a request He made—to fill the six jars! That was no minor request. Nothing is mentioned of them complaining or saying the task was too difficult. They accepted their roles to serve, and they persevered in their task. It must have taken a long time to fill the jars to the brim. We may see it as a simple task, yet it must have taken hours. They carried a lot of weight with them, but the work paid off. Jesus had turned simple well water into wine —the best wine the master of the banquet had tasted!

What was true for God's people in the Old and New Testaments is just as true for us now. This miracle-working Savior is the same One who has called us to be fathers, even though we didn't have fathers. Sometimes the calling seems very difficult. We may be carrying a lot of weight in the baggage we brought into our relationships. Yet we can find comfort in what Jesus did with the weight the wedding servants carried with them. He changed the ordinary into extraordinary. He made the best from something simple.

Like the servants, we need to persevere in our calling, sometimes struggling with the load but knowing that our Father sees the big picture. He wants to bring out His best in us. The will of the Father is for us to be filled to the brim with the Living Water of Jesus Christ, to search for His voice and listen to Him speaking words of guidance in His Word. He places godly fathers around us to be examples as we mirror the Father's ways.

Maybe you're carrying a sin that's weighing you down. Bring it to the Miracle Worker, and get ready for the miracle of forgiveness as you come in repentance. Jesus Christ brought a gift to the needy family at the wedding. He also brings the ultimate gifts to you and me—to the world—as He responds to our needs: Salvation. Forgiveness. Life. Victory. The best of the best. God the Father gave the gift of himself to a world watered down with sin.

Be patient as the Father shapes you into His best. God's timing is not ours. There is a celebration He wants us to take part in! Enjoy the blessings! Sometimes it may be easy to celebrate outwardly, yet inwardly we may be dealing with feelings of emptiness, concern, guilt, worries, and watered-down commitments as fathers. Amidst our whining, moaning, and inward groaning, Jesus hears us say to Him, "I've run out of _____" (fill in the blank as it pertains to your life). Having said that, wait for the transformation, the rejuvenation, the wisdom you need to be the best father you can be. You may not see the change at first. But you'll probably begin to notice it in your child's hug, your wife's eyes, or your priorities as they begin to change.

Let's explore one more situation in which a group of people were left without something. We find the story in Matt. 14:13-21; Mark 6:32-44; Luke 9:10-17; and John 6:1-13.

Jesus was worn out. It had been a tough couple of days. Consider some of the following responsibilities He carried: His teaching schedule had increased to full-time. He planned, prepared, and sent the 12 disciples out with a mission to preach the news about His kingdom, heal the sick, raise the dead, cleanse the lepers, and drive out demons. When they returned, He was able to briefly touch base with them, but His schedule was very crowded. Then He received word that His cousin John had been murdered. There was little time to grieve. Things were so busy that there wasn't time to eat. While attempting to find some quiet, restful time, He found the crowds following Him. So, having compassion on them, He healed their sick and began to teach them of His Father's kingdom.

Have you had those kinds of days and weeks? Your schedule can hardly fit on your calendar. Your workload is incredibly heavy. You skip some meals because sometimes there doesn't seem to be time even to eat. Throw in a personal tragedy, and you're starting to feel your limits being stretched. Quiet time would be a luxury you can ill afford, especially when you find out your child is sick. At home, you put on more hats. Husband. Father. Neighbor. Homework helper. Dishwasher. Bedtime storyteller. Mr. Fix-it.

Is it over yet? It wasn't for Jesus. And it probably won't be for you either. In Jesus' case, evening approached, and so did the disciples. A crowd of around 5,000 men plus all the women and children had gathered, and they were hungry. The disciples told Jesus "Send the crowds away, so they can go to the villages and buy themselves some food" (Matt. 14:15). But Jesus surprised them again, saying, "They do not need to go away. You give them something to eat" (v. 16). Picture the disciple's response. They must have thought Jesus had gone off the deep end. How on earth were they supposed to feed them?

The problem was that the disciples were more in awe of the crowd than with the power of Jesus Christ. I think we've all been there. We're so awed by our crowded lives that we fail to be in awe of the power of the Father, His Son, and the Holy Spirit. We hold out for overtime pay at work when we could have been home holding our children. We try to steal moments on the phone to touch base with our boss instead of attending our daughter's ballgame to watch her steal second base. You know the stories as well as I do. And listen to the rest of the story about Jesus and the crowd. . . .

The disciples found a boy with five loaves of bread and two fish. Jesus asked for them. He held them heavenward and prayed to His Father. You may be familiar with how the story ends. Not only was everyone fed, but afterward the disciples picked up 12 basketfuls of broken pieces that were left over.

The lessons seem obvious:

- When something is placed into the hands of Jesus, miracles will happen.
- When Jesus tells you to do something, don't underestimate His power to work through your life to accomplish His goal.
- Regularly spend time with Jesus. Bring your family.
- Teach your family, as Jesus has taught you, about bringing others to Him.
- Hold your children in your arms as well as up in prayer.
- Don't miss Jesus because of busyness in your life.
- Desire a passion for compassion within your home, work, and community.
- Leftovers from the hand of Jesus are more satisfying than any entree from the finest restaurant.
- The Father loves to work through His Son's words and life.

What other lessons did the Father teach you through His Son's story of the feeding of the 5,000?

_____

_____

_____

_____

_____

We've seen what the Father can do when people are without something or someone. There are many other stories to be shared as we gather as dads who did without someone special in our lives—the man we call Dad. But the Father has other specific words of promise for the fatherless. When I was young I vaguely remember my mom putting some of the following verses in my mind. Over the years, the Holy Spirit moved them from my head to my heart. With the Spirit's help, I hold on to these promises set forth in Scripture because I know God does not lie. Nor will He go back on His promises.

I want to encourage you to place gifts of Scripture in the lives of your children as my mom did. At the time it may seem to make little difference to them, but as that gift is planted there, the Holy Spirit can move those words of encouragement, hope, help, and grace from their heads to their hearts. God's Word planted in a Spirit-cultivated heart produces an abundant harvest of fruit.

As you read the promises following, ask the Holy Spirit to write them in your heart. They will bring you strength and hope as you *grace*fully father your children, following the heavenly Father's lead.

⌒

The LORD your God is God of gods and Lord of lords, the great God, mighty and awesome. . . . He defends the cause of the fatherless and the widow, and loves the alien, giving him food and clothing (Deut. 10:17-18).

Sing to God, sing praise to his name, extol him who rides on the clouds—his name is the LORD—and rejoice before him. A father to the fatherless, a defender of widows, is God in his holy dwelling (Ps. 68:4-5).

Do not move an ancient boundary stone or encroach on the fields of the fatherless, for their Defender is strong; he will take up their case against you. Apply your heart to instruction and your ears to words of knowledge (Prov. 23:10-12).

God is in your corner.
He goes to bat for the fatherless.
He stands in defense of the boundary lines of your calling to fatherhood.
God is your help and hope.
He is a Father to the fatherless.

Your Turn

○ How did the stories of the Father responding to those who were without something affect your thoughts concerning what He can do in your role as a father without a father?

○ What are the crowded areas of your life that cause you to take your focus off of the Father and off of your children? How do you plan to start standing in awe of God and His blessings?

- What or who are you going to place into the hands of Jesus? What is your prayer to the Father as you do so?
- Which of the three Bible passages at the end of the chapter means the most to you? Why?
- Will your prayers change this week? In what way?
- Do you have the desire to teach your children something that the Father taught you through this chapter? What is it?
- Choose a meaningful Bible verse with your child and memorize it together. Then pray that the Holy Spirit will move it from your heads to your hearts.

_____

_____

_____

_____

_____

_____

_____

_____

_____

_____

_____

_____

_____

_____

_____

_____

"The world is full of so-called prayer warriors who are prayer-ignorant. They're full of formulas and programs and advice, peddling techniques for getting what you want from God. Don't fall for that nonsense. This is your Father you are dealing with, and he knows better than you what you need. With a God like this loving you, you can pray very simply. Like this:

'Our Father in heaven,
Reveal who you are.
Set the world right;
Do what's best –
    as above, so below.
Keep us alive with three square meals
Keep us forgiven with you and forgiving others.
Keep us safe from ourselves and the Devil.
You're in charge!
You can do anything you want!
You're ablaze in beauty!
    Yes. Yes. Yes.'"

— Jesus, stepson of Joseph, also Son of God the Father
(Matt. 6:7-13, TM)

5

Missed Out on Father-to-Father Talks?
The Importance of Prayer

As I was growing up I always began my personal prayers with "Dear Heavenly Father." I always called God "Father." I did that on purpose. It helped me remember that although I was fatherless in the earthly sense, I had a Heavenly Father who was always with me. While my prayer names for addressing God change now with the situation, "Father" is still the most meaningful. As mentioned in the previous chapter, being fatherless has made it difficult for some to see God as Father.

As you draw closer to the Father through His Son, Jesus Christ, I pray you'll be able to draw great strength from knowing you have a perfect Father. One of the great bonuses of having a Father who loves and cares for you is the time spent in father-to-father talks, which are also Father-to-son talks.

When I became a father for the first time, I longed for a father who would give me advice on parenting, remind me of things we did together, and share the common joy of fatherhood.

Although that didn't and won't happen in one sense, I'm so thankful for a Heavenly Father who has an entire Book of advice for me on parenting—the Bible. He reminds me of things we went through together over the years. And He shares that common joy of fatherhood with me as He loves being the perfect Father to all of His children.

One of the greatest gifts God has entrusted to our care is prayer—a 24/7/365 open line of communication for father-to-Father talks with no long distance charges, because He's always beside you. If your desire is to be a better father to your children, set your heart on being a dad who prays.

Don't let human excuses get in the way of communicating with the Divine. Forget generation gaps, different interests, fear of speaking (praying) out loud, pride, or lack of interest. Your Heavenly Father wants to guide you into every decision you face as a father. He will give you His undivided attention. He wants only the best for you and your family. And on top of it all, He promises to answer—according to His perfect will, ways, and timing, which you can fully trust.

Prayers by fathers who desire to be the best fathers they can for their children begin with words of repentance. Have you asked your Heavenly Father to forgive your failures as His child and as a father to the children He entrusted to your care? Start there. Then go to your child and ask him or her for forgiveness for anything that may need to be forgiven. If you can't do that just yet, go back to the Father and ask that your pride be crushed and your heart be opened to admit your failings. It's a powerful gift for both you and your child to confess your sins and to receive each other's forgiveness.

God's Word guides us into this confessional mode in the verse below, noted in two different translations of the Bible plus my own paraphrase:

○ "Confess your sins to each other and pray for each other so that you may be healed. The prayer of a righteous man is powerful and effective" (James 5:16).

- "Make this your common practice: Confess your sins to each other and pray for each other so that you can live together whole and healed. The prayer of a person living right with God is something powerful to be reckoned with" (James 5:16, TM).
- "The prayer of a father who seeks the Father's heart for His children is powerful and effective" (latter part of James 5:16, author's paraphrase).

Having the ultimate father to talk to at any and all times is a magnificent gift for all dads. He serves up guidance, peace, and wisdom as we come to Him in prayer.

Rom. 8:26-28 is one of my favorite passages in the Bible. For you who don't know exactly what to pray or what to pray for yourself and your children, let these words soak into your mind and heart:

> If we don't know how or what to pray, it doesn't matter. He does our praying in and for us, making prayer out of our wordless sighs, our aching groans. He knows us far better than we know ourselves . . . and keeps us present before God. That's why we can be so sure that every detail in our lives of love for God is worked into something good (TM).

Not only must we realize the importance of prayer in our lives—we're also called to teach our children to pray. How are our children going to learn to pray or see its value and life-changing importance if they don't see or hear us praying? In Luke 11:1 the disciples said to Jesus, "Lord, teach us to pray." He taught them the words to what we call "The Lord's Prayer."

In teaching our children to pray, we need to let them hear what's on our hearts; what's going on in our days; our love for the Lord; how to forgive; how to intercede for others; and how to give God all the glory and praise in all things. Prayers shared between parent and child (or any relationship) will strengthen the bond of love. It's a sharing of hearts with the Father's heart.

A wonderful way to lift your children up to the Father's throne of grace is to pray Scripture for them and over them. Take a verse or passage and at the appropriate places insert your child's name. Make scripture personal. Make the verse a specific prayer. Share the prayer with your children. Give them a passage and ask them to pray it for you. The following are examples of praying scripture (insert your child's name in the blank):

Show _____ your ways, O LORD, teach _____ your paths; guide _____ in your truth . . . and may _____'s hope be in you all day long (Ps. 25:4-5, author's paraphrase).

Hide _____ in the shelter of your presence from the intrigues of men; keep him [her] safe from accusing tongues (Ps. 31:20, author's paraphrase).

Help _____ to love righteousness and hate wickedness (Ps. 45:7, author's paraphrase).

May _____ love the Lord with all his [her] heart and with all his [her] soul and with all his [her] mind (Matt. 22:37, author's paraphrase).

Guide _____'s feet into the path of peace (Luke 1:79, author's paraphrase).

Protect _____ from the evil one (John 17:15, author's paraphrase).

Give _____ the strength to obey God rather than men (Acts 5:29, author's paraphrase).

May _____ be joyful always, pray continually, and give thanks in all circumstances (1 Thess. 5:16-18, author's paraphrase).

May _____ have a pure heart, good conscience, and sincere faith (1 Tim. 1:5, author's paraphrase).

The night before Jesus gave His life, He spent time alone with his closest friends, the disciples. Toward the end of the evening He took the time to pray to His Father. The prayer is known as the high-priestly prayer because Jesus was interceding to the Father on behalf of others. The prayer is in three parts. As we consider the quest as great fathers to serve our children, Jesus' prayer (recorded in John 17) would be a nice format for our prayers. First, Jesus prayed for himself. There's nothing wrong with praying for our own needs as we ask God to bring out His best in us. Then He prayed for those closest to him—His students, the disciples. We need to pray for those who are learning to be parents under our tutelage—our children. And finally Jesus prays for all believers. Let's pray for each other! What a strengthening gift to know that other fatherless fathers are praying for us.

Here's a starter list of suggestions as we pray for ourselves. Since everyone's specific needs will differ, the following is a general topical list.

Lift yourself up before the throne of grace

Dear Father,

May my faith in the one true God—Father, Son, and Holy Spirit—grow, and my faithful example show.

Lead the relationship I have with my children, that it be guided and strengthened by You, the Father of all fathers.

Set my priorities according to Your Word, not the world. Align my will with Yours.

Show me the joy of Your salvation in my everyday life.

Teach me to forgive as You have forgiven me.

Give me grace in dealing with, thinking about, and understanding my father.

Grant that I may love my spouse [ex-wife or other parental

*relationship] in a way that is pleasing to You and leaves a
healthy imprint on the lives of our children.*
(Add to the list)

_____

_____

_____

Here's a starter prayer list as we intercede for our children. Since everyone's specific needs for his or her children
will differ, the following is a general topical list.

Lift up your children in prayer regarding these topics:

A faith in Christ that won't bend
A strong father-child relationship
A deep prayer life
Future spouse/family
Purity in relationships
Joy in being a Christian
Respect for God, His people, and His creation
A compassionate heart
Identification of spiritual gifts and use of them to the
    fullest
Wisdom
A forgiving, graceful heart
Integrity
Christian friends
Joy in being a witness of Jesus Christ
Health
Selfless attitude
Humility
Self-control
A church home that's Christ centered and Spirit led
Power to withstand temptation
Healing for past hurts

Self-worth found in Jesus ("Christ-esteem," not self-
esteem)
(Add to the list)

_____

_____

_____

_____

_____

_____

_____

Here's a starter prayer list as we intercede for other fathers.

Let us pray for fathers . . .

. . . who are out of work and those who are out of control.

. . . raising stepchildren and those working on raising the level of integrity in their lives.

. . . feeling overburdened who need to unburden their concerns on the Lord.

. . . building a new home and those struggling to build a savings account.

. . . striving to imitate Christ and those who are not intimate with their wives.

. . . coping with thoughts of divorce and those having difficulty coping after divorce.

. . . in physical pain and those trying to keep from causing physical pain.

. . . grieving a loss and those rejoicing at finding God's eternal promises of life.

. . . dealing with aging and others dealing with aging parents.

. . . feeling lost and those who seem to have lost compassionate feelings.

. . . who are honoring their wives and families and in turn are honoring God.

. . . growing in their faith and others who are dying due to lack of faith.

. . . ministering to other families and families who are ministering to fathers.

. . . traveling on business and those who are busy traveling back to God's ways.

. . . who aren't able to see their children and children who don't know their fathers.

. . . expecting a child and those expecting other kinds of miracles.

. . . battling diseases or handicaps and all fathers battling the disease of sin.

. . . who easily lose their patience and fathers who are doctors treating patients.

. . . learning to worship in Spirit and truth and those who have difficulty telling the truth.

. . . burdened by guilt and those freed by God's forgiveness.

. . . behind prison walls and those living in other kinds of sin-imposed prisons.

. . . putting work before God and family and those working at putting God first.

. . . addicted to substances and others who are working at a substantive friendship.

. . . dealing with the empty-nest syndrome and those with an empty-heart syndrome.

. . . rejoicing in their children's accomplishments and those accomplishing the joyful task of teaching their children to rejoice in all circumstances.

. . . in the middle of a midlife crisis and those in the middle of a midday prayer.

. . . putting their children through school and those putting themselves through school.

. . . who are teenagers and those with children who are teenagers.

. . . who pray and are strengthened by knowing others are praying for them.

(Add to the list)

_____

_____

_____

_____

_____

_____

_____

Your Turn

Who taught you to pray? How do you usually address the Lord in your prayers? What have you learned from the Heavenly Father about being a father? What would you like to learn from him? Is there something that is keeping you from praying more, praying with your children, praying aloud, or praying with others? How do you plan to use the suggestions in this chapter regarding your prayer life—your father-to-Father talks? What do you want to teach your children about prayer? When do you plan to start teaching them?

_____

_____

_____

_____

Often the deepest relationships can be developed during the simplest activities.

—Gary Smalley

My mother and father divorced when my twin brother and I were less than a year old. I only have a few vague images of my father, mainly of being transported back and forth for visitations. I don't remember anything we actually did together. There was another woman in his life.

I do carry with me the impression that I wasn't a priority in his life. When I was older, my mother told me he refused to hold me as a baby because I was named after my maternal grandfather.

Growing up without a father seemed normal; you don't miss what you never had. Mom always had time and affection for us. I was never bitter toward my father. Even if I didn't have a good model for a father, I at least had an example of what to avoid. I had all kinds of fears concerning becoming an adult, finding a wife, and having children. My doubts kept me up at night as I poured out my heart to God. Although I have a strong Christian faith now, I am ashamed to say I didn't trust, understand, or even know the Lord back then. Long before I turned my life over to Jesus, He was there protecting and providing for me in ways I could never imagine.

My advice to fathers? Spend half as much money and twice as much time. That's what kids want, and that's what they need.

—W. B.

6

Is Commitment an Issue?
The Importance of Giving Your Heart

Your father walked out on you and your family when you were seven years old. He just up and left. Maybe he thought he had done his time. Maybe things changed and he just didn't want the hassles anymore.

Fast forward. Your child is seven years old. You're under scrutiny at work, bill collectors are hounding you, and the relationship with your wife is well beyond the honeymoon stage, to say the least.

Your father walked out. He wasn't committed to the relationships in his house. What's going to be different in your house? The example left behind for you is not a good or godly one.

Many fatherless fathers have a problem committing to marriage, father-child relationships, or jobs, because they never observed commitment in action when they were children. We live what we know. We learn about marriage from the marriage relationship we witnessed on a regular basis. We learn about parenting from the parent figures we had in our lives.

If you struggle with commitment because of broken relationships in your life, you need to know that the cycle can be broken. It starts with a heart that desires to beat in sync with the heart of the Heavenly Father, who is totally committed to you. In a simplistic way, it could also be said that you simply have to make the decision to put your heart into loving your family. Unfortunately, it's not always that easy, especially for fathers who carry heavy baggage from their childhood.

You're no doubt aware of the fact that women who were abused as children often find themselves married to an abuser. And children of alcoholics easily end up as adults in relationships with alcoholics. It seems to defy right thinking. But it happens daily to intelligent people who hated what they had growing up yet end up in the same situations as adults. We live what we know. We're drawn to what we know and were taught as a child. We're conditioned into thinking there's no other way. But the cycle *can* be broken. A power exists that's greater than the deceptions that bombard us.

Those first years of our lives are so important and play an amazingly vital part in who we are as adults. But the negatives can be changed to positives, and the positives can be reinforced in our lives if we choose to take that route. I imagine you do since you are reading these pages. For example, for those who were abandoned by a father or for those whose parents divorced, being totally committed to being a good father—one who meets his family's spiritual, emotional, and physical needs—may be the number-one priority. I write this with that hope. Giving your heart to your children can start by taking a diagnostic test regarding how committed your heart is to God. A recommitment to the Heavenly Father may be the first step in giving your heart fully to your family. Fortunately, we have a God who is slow to anger and abounding in love and forgiveness.

Are you ready to be totally committed to your family? Maybe a better question is—Are you ready to be totally committed to your Father in heaven, who gives the power, wisdom, and love needed for you to give your all to your family?

How are you going to deal with the lack of your father's

commitment or the lack of your father's presence in your life? With so many different situations, it's impossible to address them all. Let me throw out the following general thoughts, and you can apply them, as best suited, to your situation:

○ Is forgiveness a gift you need to give to your father? How can that be accomplished? Don't let pride get in the way. See the gift as a way for you to find joy and commitment in your role as a father. If you're no longer able to share that forgiveness face to face, write it out or talk it out in private. Forgive as the Lord has forgiven you. Forgiveness doesn't mean saying what happened is OK. It's not. But forgiveness does involve letting go of the burden you're carrying. Start fresh as you allow God to lift the anger, resentment, bitterness, and loneliness from your heart. Don't focus on what you missed out on but rather on what you can enjoy with your own children. Set aside regrets and start gracefully and joyfully molding the lives of your own children. This is a legacy that can be passed on for generations to come.

○ If you need to seek the help of others, don't put it off. God has placed wonderful Christian counselors, pastors, and wise friends around you who can offer practical means to enable you to recommit your life to your family.

○ Seek help from committed fathers whom God has placed around you. They may be in your family, workplace, or neighborhood. Don't shy away from taking their advice or just watching and learning how they give their hearts to their children. Observe how they carry out their commitment as fathers, and apply it to your life.

○ Commitment to your family may mean commitment

to changing ways, lifestyles, or habits that are hurting your relationships. Are you honestly ready to deal with what needs to be changed?

o Take time to read parenting materials that can help mold you into a better-equipped father. Men will spend time and money on their personal hobbies and interests. Unfortunately, some men don't spend a fraction of that time, money, and energy on what's really important—faith and family. Take advantage of the many great books, videos, DVDs, and maga-zines available at Christian bookstores, through on-line distributors, or at the library. Your children will want your help with the issues they're facing as they grow up. These resources can often be beneficial.

o You may find the need in your area (through work, church, and so on) for fathers to come together to talk, encourage each other in their commitment, and share resources. Maybe you're the person to start such a group. If your church has a men's group, en-courage a retreat for fatherless fathers. Maybe you can start a prayer chain for others coming from simi-lar situations. These groups can help you find great joy in prioritizing your activities and giving your heart to your children.

o Read the Bible. There you find the kind of commit-ment that God is calling you to make to Him and to others. But it's the gospel (good news) message of Jesus Christ that's going to give you the proper motivation to make a commitment to your Savior and to your family whom He saved by giving His heart—His all.

Your Turn

As you grew up, what events or people shaped your in-terests, ways, views, and commitments? Which of those are good and godly, and what do you want to change so that you can be fully committed to your God and family? If you need to forgive your father for something, how do you plan to go about that? If there is no way to get in touch with him, write what you might say to him to move beyond hurt to a life committed to your children.

_____

_____

_____

_____

_____

_____

_____

_____

_____

_____

_____

_____

_____

_____

_____

_____

_____

_____

_____

_____

_____

The best thing to spend on your child is your time.

—Arnold Glasgow

I was born in February of 1944, and my father was killed in Europe in November of that same year. Naturally, I have no recollections of my father.

My mother remarried in 1948, and my brother and I were subsequently adopted by our stepfather, and a sister was born to us from that union.

My stepfather was a good man and good to my mother, but not much of a parent, not even to his own daughter. I don't remember even having an extended conversation with him, and he died just two years ago. My childhood memories are of us having to be quiet when Dad came home because he worked hard and had to sit in his chair and watch television until bedtime. On vacations he went fishing by himself all day while the rest of us did something else.

He did other things to alienate my brother and me. The name of our birth father was never spoken in his presence. Pictures were stashed away. He never mentioned to anyone that we were adopted, although Mom did.

—Karl

7

Making Up for Lost Talk Time
The Importance of Communicating with Your Children

I never heard my father's voice. And he never heard mine. He never had the opportunity to sit me down for a man-to-man talk. As I talk to my children, I can't help but wonder if that's how he would have talked to me. How would I want my father to talk to me? Am I respecting my children's ideas and ways as I would have wanted him to respect mine?

The Family Initiative Council wrote in one of their brochures that fathers spend an average of 39 seconds a day talking to their children. Thirty-nine seconds! Ouch! We can't let that stand. Communication with our children must be a high priority.

In striving to be a good dad when you didn't have one, the simplest question to answer in regard to communicating with your children is "What would you have wanted to talk to your dad about as you grew up?" The answers will vary as we consider the various ages and stages of our childhood, but I think it's the right question to get us thinking.

At the same time, realize that children are not always comfortable talking to their parents, especially if there's been a divorce and they have trust issues or if your relationship with them has been strained in the past. It may take time. But look for what Gail McDonald calls "open window moments." Those are the times when children open up a shade and say, "Here I am—look inside." Those moments might be at bedtime, when they are sick, in the midst of a difficult, frightening, or exhilarating time. Sometimes the open window moment might come at night, in the dark—inside or outside—since children may open up more if they don't have to look directly into your eyes. Be aware of these moments when God opens the window for you and your child.

If you and God are in the midst of repairing a difficult relationship with your son or daughter, the place to begin communicating may be with two short words: "I'm sorry." Another phrase that's a great healer is "I love you." Those are foundational words for building a relationship that includes great communication. Children have to trust you before opening up their world to you. If you've broken that trust, forgiveness needs to be granted.

And why is it that so many men have trouble saying, "I love you?" Many of us are getting better at it—we're probably much farther down the road of showing affection than many of our parents, but we have a long way to go. "I love you" can change your child's day and probably many areas of their lives. So many men, women, and children have longed to hear their fathers say those three words. It's a simple phrase packed with importance, confidence, and power.

If you're looking for a communication starting point, get to know your child's interests. So what is his or her world like? What kind of music does he or she listen to? What's *in*? What's *out*?

One-on-one time is a wonderful gift for your children. Have a "date night" with your daughter or a "boys' night out" with your son. Talk. Laugh. Get to know your children in a different light.

It can also be amazingly important for your children to know your story. Do they know who you are? Do they know what you actually go through at work? What about the things you struggle with on a daily basis or in general? What about faith issues? Do they know your inward thoughts about being raised without a father? Do you think they realize you struggle at times wanting to be a good dad while not having that example from your own life? This, too, can be a valuable gift to share with your children at the right time and maturity level. By opening your heart, you open the door for your children to reveal their hearts to you.

If you're divorced and only get to spend time with your children during assigned visits, don't turn it into a 24/7 playtime complete with gifts at Dad's theme park. This type of treatment is usually motivated out of guilt, not love. And as much fun as the time may be, children will see through it. Their deeper desire is to just spend time with a dad who cares about them—what they're doing and where they're headed. They want a dad who loves them, not a circus ringmaster.

If communication with your children is forced and awkward, look for other open windows. Don't force it. Respect them, but don't give up. Build up the trust. Find little openings where the talking starts to flow. And be a good listener. Listening creates trust. Trust is what relationships are built on.

We all may have missed out on some great father-son talks growing up, but we have a lifetime to see that things will be different for our children.

I remember being intrigued as a child by a factory being built near my house. I was amazed at how the crew worked together to create this building where every beam, nail, and wire ended up right where it needed to be.

Until that experience, the only other construction site I had ever "visited" was during Sunday School. I remember that we took a Bible "trip" to a site called Babel. People gathered there to build a city by themselves, including a tower that reached to the heavens. They built it to make a name for themselves, but their plan had some major problems: they had forgotten to include an Architect in their plans—the One who had designed and created a once-flawless world. Their second mistake was that they tried to build it *by* themselves *for* themselves. They wanted the glory, the power, and a great name.

God decided to include himself in their selfish plans. He came down and confused their language so they could not understand each other. A proper, safe, and sturdy building can't be built without communicating.

We spend a lot of time at a construction site. God is constructing our Christian homes. He's the Architect, and He's using us as His builders. The foundation is built on Jesus Christ. He needs us to work together in building this Christian home for our family. He has the plans laid out clearly on paper—it's an inspired plan. We have His Word on it! The materials used are to only be the best of love, honesty, trust, joy, respect, peace, and honor. Daily we're to be working on the holy ground of this construction site, where our Christian home is being built.

As our home is being constructed, Satan notices what's happening. His desire is to halt our progress. He borrows a plan similar to the one God used at Babel. He causes communication problems within the home—the construction site. He tempts us with a sinful breakdown of communication between Mom and Dad, parents and children, brothers and sisters, between our families and the Architect and Builder, Jesus Christ.

When communication breaks down within a Christian home, the construction work is broken down as well. Sometimes Satan confuses our language, causing us not to honor each other. Often he plugs our ears so that we fail to listen to each other. He tries his best to cause us to fail to communicate with God and tempts us to focus on ourselves and off our God.

We must fight this spiritual warfare with prayer and the power of the Holy Spirit. Realize that Jesus Christ has already won the victory over Satan for us through His life, death, and resurrection. Pray for angel guards to surround your home so Satan can't tempt you to halt construction of your Christian home. And pray that angels are also sent to open up hearts and mouths so that your home is one where communication freely flows, where God talk is free and comfortable, where the truth spoken in love flows from room to room, and where praise breaks forth from everyone in the home as well as from every room, beam, mortar, and garden!

Your Turn

How would you rate your communication skills or time with your children on a scale of 1 to 10? List specific ways you plan to improve your one-on-one talk time with your children. What areas of their lives do you need to get to know?

_____

_____

_____

_____

_____

_____

_____

_____

_____

_____

_____

The lap: that wide playground space along the body's front. The lap represents a very special place in fathers, because it is the first place most dads play with their kids. Here is where the deepest roots of love are made. O lap, o place of holy tryst, do we ever stare at other things the way we do at our kids in our lap?
　　　　　　　　　—Patch Adams, *Being a Father—Family, Work, and Self*

I was only seven years old when my father passed away. But in the short amount of time that we spent together, he raised me the right way. I always knew he loved me very much. I wish my father were alive today so that he could enjoy everything that God has given to me. Another regret that I have is that I never got a chance to have a catch with my father. I didn't start playing baseball until I was 14. My brother Luis was the one who played, and he introduced me to the game.
　　　　　　　　　　　　　　　—Sammy Sosa
　　　　　　　　　　　　　　　In Jonathan P. Decker,
　　　　　　　　　　　Great Dads—A Celebration of Fatherhood

I am passionate about silliness, and my sons have enhanced that in me from the beginning.
　　　　　　　　　　　　　　　—Patch Adams

8

Wish You Had More Laughter Instead of Tears?
The Importance of Having Fun

The movie *Field of Dreams* is a favorite of mine. The ending especially gets to me because, yes, I wonder what it would be like to play catch with my dad. Special emotions are stirred in me when I attend a baseball game with my children. Would my dad have taken me—just the two of us—to games? I hope he would have.

It may not be a baseball game, but many of you reading this have had similar dreams. Too many of your childhood homes were filled with fearful tears rather than laughter. Fatherhood fun may sound like an oxymoron to you. Maybe you grew up in a strict home in which fun was to be left at school. That may have shaped you into the man you are today. For your child's sake, I would like to make this profound statement: "Lighten up!"

Maybe it's time you let your children teach you about playtime. Play! Laugh! Enjoy your children! Act like a kid! Let them explore God's creation with creativity. Not only is laughter and joy good for the soul, but humor can be a great catalyst for health and healing. Healing may be just what you need as you recover from a childhood that wasn't the way God planned.

According to one humorist, or "jolly-tologist," adults average 15 laughs a day, while children laugh 400 times a day. Somewhere between childhood and adulthood, we

lose 385 laughs a day! That's a great loss! Maybe we need
not only the faith of a child but the funny bone of one as
well!

Smack dab in the middle of all the stress and problems
you may have in your life right now, God has given you the
wonderful gift of children. And children know how to have
fun. They love to play. They love to laugh. In fact, is there
any better sound than that of a giggling child? They are
masters of silliness. But somewhere in maturing from childhood to adulthood, too many fathers received the wrong
message that good, clean, roll-down-the-hill, laugh-till-it-
hurts fun must end when you have children. Learn from
your children. Accept the gift of joy from your Heavenly
Father. Leave your work at the office, your boring attitude
at the doorstep, your problems at the Cross, and enjoy your
children. Turn your home into a haven of joy. Introduce
laughter to mealtimes. Bring home tickles from work. Allow peaceful bedtime stories to get out of hand, turning into wired and wild gigglefests. Create the World Cup in
your backyard. Produce off-off-off Broadway theatrical
events in your basement. Or just sit down and enjoy a good
old-fashioned comedy on television.

Even though I didn't get to sit in my father's lap for a
bedtime story, I was privileged to have had the experience
of crawling into the lap of my Heavenly Father for a good
read—He's an author, you know! Read to your children.
Make that a lasting memory of fun. Act out the story. Create unforgettable characters as you change your voice.
Don't inhibit or stifle the creativity with which God has
blessed you.

The possibilities for fun in your home are endless.
The message is clear. Children raised in a house filled with
joy and laughter are happier and emotionally healthier
throughout their lives. And they take with them to school,

the neighborhood, and into adulthood a joy that's contagious.

If your joy level seems to be dead on arrival when you pass through the doors of your home, first take on the prayer of David during a time in his life when guilt and sin had robbed him of his joy. His words found in Ps. 51:12 read, "Restore to me the joy of your salvation and grant me a willing spirit, to sustain me."

Not surprisingly, the source of joy goes back to the Cross and your salvation through Jesus Christ. David was saved by grace through faith in his Lord. Connected to that salvation was the cross of Jesus Christ, the promised Messiah who would come centuries down the road. David had known the joy of the Lord but was now burdened by sin and its accompanying guilt. Maybe you were once filled with laughter that has since been silenced for some reason. Or possibly that has never been a part of your life because of the hurts and abuse of a broken family. David's prayer and yours can be the same: "Restore to me the joy of your salvation."

Too many people think following Jesus Christ is a road that leads to boredom, rules, and a definite lack of joy. The opposite is true. With Christ comes true joy. The chains of legalism are broken, and people are freed to a world of happiness. Nehemiah declared to God's people, "Do not grieve, for the joy of the LORD is your strength" (Neh. 8:10). Jesus said to his disciples, "I have come that they may have life, and have it to the full" (John 10:10).

Imagine growing up in a home with parents who were filled with joy and laughter, a home in which all the family members knew and lived life to the fullest—the abundant life Jesus Christ came to give. Now that's a home we all would like to have grown up in. Don't you think that's the kind of home life your children would love to experience?

What's stopping you? The gift of joy is readily available from your Father in heaven. Just ask. What's keeping you?

Father, restore to me the joy of Your salvation. Father, restore my home to the joy that comes first and foremost from the joy of knowing You love me and have saved me. Father, I lay my burdens at Your cross as I head out to find my children . . . to play!

Your Turn

What is holding back the laughter in your life? How do you plan to change that? List some specific ideas you have for bringing fun, laughter, or silliness into your child's life this week.

_____

_____

_____

_____

_____

_____

_____

_____

_____

_____

_____

_____

_____

_____

_____

_____

You'll make a lot of mistakes in your life. . . . But if you learn from every mistake, you really didn't make a mistake.
—Vince Lombardi

I don't mind looking in the mirror and seeing my father.
—Michael Douglas

9

Mirror, Mirror on the Wall
The Importance of Being Yourself

My wife was nine months pregnant with our first child when a sense of concern close to fear hit me. I was about to become a father, and I didn't know how to handle it. I never had a father living in my home, so how was I supposed to know how to act, what to do, and tell right from wrong regarding dadhood?

When I shared my concerns with my wife, Chiara, I remember her advice word for word. That's because it was straightforward and simple. She said, "Just be yourself."

That sounds too easy—doesn't it? She had confidence in who I was and that I would be a good dad to our children if I just continued being the person God had raised me to be. There is great importance in being yourself as you grow as a father to your children.

Some of you may be thinking, *You don't know me. I've messed things up with my children, and I don't want to continue being myself.* We've all been in that boat of not liking who we are or where we've been. That's why we need to see ourselves as Christ sees us—redeemed, forgiven people. Forgiveness changes lives—ours and those of our children.

This isn't a matter of self-esteem. It's a matter of Christ-esteem. If we only look at ourselves, without Christ living within us, then we'll see failures. We'll see men who can't possibly be the dads we want to be. We'll continually fail. But when we have Christ-esteem, we see our Savior's love, strength, and joy living within us. We find forgiveness for our past mistakes and hope for the future. Everything changes when Jesus Christ covers our lives. Then we can all agree with confidence that just being ourselves is important as we daily follow the call to be dads.

What if you look in the mirror and see an alcoholic? Or a deadbeat dad who wants to change but has burned many bridges? Or a man who was abandoned as a child and followed in his father's footsteps? What if the mirror reminds you that you haven't even come close to being a spiritual leader for your family?

First of all, be assured that your Father in heaven loves you. He hasn't given up on you, even if it seems everyone else has. Second, know that your lifestyle is not aligned with the will of God. Like any parent, he loves you but hates the sinful action.

Next, be grateful that God has shown you a clear reflection of yourself and that you've accepted the fact that the image in the glass is really you. That's called facing reality. If you need to admit that you've failed in many ways as a father, so be it. Admit it. Confess it. Take it to the ultimate Father—the One who gives second, third, and fourth chances, the One who forgives and wipes the slate clean.

Then go to your family you have hurt and ask for their forgiveness. You may have hurt them deeply, and moving on will most likely not be instantaneous. You have broken a trust with them, and you have to win that back. With God's help, continue to make amends in all areas of your life. Get involved in a Christ-centered church and a Bible study or small group. God may work through Alcoholics Anonymous, Gamblers Anonymous, Narcotics Anonymous, or other addiction groups to help you, depending on your need.

It's going to take time and work. Commitment is always a factor in building a good, healthy relationship with children. Take an honest look in the mirror, into your heart, and into the heart of God as you climb the steps of dadhood that lead to a higher goal.

It's also beneficial to stop many times during each month and try to take an account of how you're doing as a father. Note the highs and lows, the need for confession and forgiveness, as well as how much time is being spent with family compared to other responsibilities.

Our lives have all been changed in powerful ways by growing up without a father or having been raised with a father who wasn't a part of our lives emotionally. And what's extraordinary about that fact is that it doesn't have the effect of a one-time event. Being fatherless changes every aspect of who each of us has become as men and as fathers. Freud described the death of his father as the most important and poignant loss of his life. Death, divorce, abandonment, incarceration, and the like create sweeping changes in our lives.

God's promise is "that in all things [He] works for the good of those who love him, who have been called according to his purpose" (Rom. 8:28). That truth is one we must believe in and hold on to as we journey through fatherhood and life in general. That changes how we view ourselves, our family, and everything we encounter in life.

Recently I encountered a situation with my older son that I didn't feel I handled in the best way. It was one of those really important fatherly decision times. Afterward, I didn't feel good about the way I dealt with it, the way I spoke to him, and the ultimate decision that was made.

I sought him out and experienced one of those great open window moments between a father and son. My wife was out, his sister and brother were already in bed, and he was lying on our bed, flipping the channels on the television set. I asked if he was watching something important or if we could talk. He was just passing time, so he turned off the television set, and I turned out the light and laid down next to him to talk in the dark. I shared from my heart that I probably didn't handle the situation in the best way. And then I took the opportunity to tell him that he was going to have to be patient with me as a father since I'm learning this role as I go along. I had no example or father figure to learn from as a child, so he would have to bear with me, I told him. Together we would grow and learn.

My son may forget that night, but I never will. I was myself and showed him who I was—blemishes and all. It's so very important to be yourself with your children—the person God has created and is constantly forming into a new and glorious creation and father, following the lead of your Heavenly Father.

Your Turn

As you look at who you are, what aspects don't you like about yourself that you want to change with God's help? Are you willing to ask for help? When you look into the mirror, what is it you're able to fully appreciate in light of your past? How does the concept of "Christ-esteem" rather than "self-esteem" change the perspective you have of yourself and others?

_____

_____

_____

_____

_____

_____

A tree cannot stand without its roots.

—Zarian proverb

I had no fears of being a father, but when my son was born, I remember a sudden rush of responsibility. (The first rush was when I was married.) In retrospect, I want my children to have the father that I never had.

I have to say that I also learned about fatherhood from God, and I truly mean it. And I do believe that it is every father's responsibility to display God's fatherhood in the way he functions in that role. I also learned more about God's fatherhood when I became a father.

—K. C.

10

The Future Isn't What It Used to Be
The Importance of a Bright Tomorrow

I've realized as I grow older (along with my children), that my desire for a father probably grows stronger rather than fades. That doesn't mean the future grows dimmer, but brighter. Every passing year causes me to realize the importance of the role I play in my children's lives. For me, moving forward means gaining ground on meeting both my Heavenly Father and my earthly father in heaven. What a peaceful joy it is to know that tomorrow will be bright no matter what happens! Hopefully, prayerfully, through this journey together, we've all learned something about being better dads even though we didn't grow up with one. Because of the blessing of our Heavenly Father, the future just isn't what it used to be. Where there once was fear, strength has prevailed. Forgiveness has replaced bitterness. Hope has overpowered hopelessness. Weakness has miraculously turned to power. And tears of sadness have become tears of joy.

I've chosen to fill this chapter with words of promise and hope from God's Word. He has changed our present and future while making us look differently at our past. The Holy Spirit wants to use the inspired words that follow to brighten the future you have with your children and your faith in God. Don't hinder the Spirit's work. Open your heart; as you do, you'll find yourself open to a new kind of love, faith, and strength that will lead you to be a good dad—a great and godly dad—even though you didn't have one.

I know the plans I have for you, declares the LORD, plans to prosper you and not to harm you, plans to give you hope and a future (Jer. 29:11).

Sing to God, sing praise to his name, extol him who rides on the clouds—his name is the LORD—and rejoice before him. A father to the fatherless, a defender of widows, is God in his holy dwelling (Ps. 68:4-5).

I lift up my eyes to the hills—where does my help come from? My help comes from the LORD, the Maker of heaven and earth. He will not let your foot slip—he who watches over you will not slumber; indeed, he who watches over Israel will neither slumber nor sleep. The LORD watches over you—the LORD is your shade at your right hand; the sun will not harm you by day, nor the moon by night. The LORD will keep you from all harm—he will watch over your life; the LORD will watch over your coming and going both now and forevermore (Ps. 121).

God is our refuge and strength, an ever-present help in trouble. . . . "Be still and know that I am God." . . . The LORD Almighty is with us; the God of Jacob is our fortress (Ps. 46:1, 10-11).

Do not fear, O Zion; do not let your hands hang limp. The LORD your God is with you, he is mighty to save. He will take great delight in you, he will quiet you with his love, he will rejoice over you with singing (Zeph. 3:16-17).

[Jesus said,] Peace I leave with you; my peace I give you. I do not give to you as the world gives. Do not let your hearts be troubled and do not be afraid (John 14:27).

[Jesus said,] I am the vine; you are the branches. If a man remains in me and I in him, he will bear much fruit; apart from me you can do nothing (John 15:5).

There is now no condemnation for those who are in Christ Jesus, because through Christ Jesus the law of the Spirit of life set me free from the law of sin and death (Rom. 8:1-2).

If God is for us, who can be against us? . . . Who shall separate us from the love of Christ? Shall trouble or hardship or persecution or famine or nakedness or danger or sword? . . . No, in all these things we are more than conquerors through him who loved us. For I am convinced that neither death nor life, neither angels nor demons, neither the present nor the future, nor any powers, neither height nor depth, nor anything else in all creation, will be able to separate us from the love of God that is in Christ Jesus our Lord (Rom. 8:31, 35, 37-39).

The fruit of the Spirit is love, joy, peace, patience, kindness, goodness, faithfulness, gentleness and self-control (Gal. 5:22-23).

Rejoice in the Lord always. I will say it again: Rejoice! Let your gentleness be evident to all. The Lord is near. Do not be anxious about anything, but in everything, by prayer and petition, with thanksgiving, present your requests to God. And the peace of God, which transcends all understanding, will guard your hearts and your minds in Christ Jesus.

Finally, brothers, whatever is true, whatever is noble, whatever is right, whatever is pure, whatever is admirable —if anything is excellent or praiseworthy—think about such things. Whatever you have learned or received or heard from me, or seen in me—put it into practice. And the God of peace will be with you. . . .

I can do everything through him who gives me strength (Phil. 4:4-9, 13).

Your Turn

Which of the preceding Scripture passages brings you the most hope and comfort? Put into words the changes you're beginning to feel about your future in regard to your relationship with yourself, your children, and your Heavenly Father.

_____

_____

_____

_____

_____

_____

_____

_____

_____

_____

_____

_____

_____

_____

_____

_____

_____

_____

_____

_____

_____

_____

_____

_____

_____

_____

_____

_____

_____

_____

_____

_____

_____

_____

_____

_____

_____

A Journal Starter

Writing the Legacy for Healthy, Happy Generations to Come

One of the things I regret about growing up without a father is that I don't know much about my dad. I would love to have more facts about who he was, his joys and frustrations, and so on. As a writer, I treasure the written word. I love the few examples I have of my father's handwriting and signature. I wish I had examples of his thoughts or experiences down in writing. I would love to read about his journey of faith. I think we as fathers need to leave a written and oral record for our children.

Based on 2 Cor. 3:3, which reads, "You show that you are a letter from Christ . . . written not with ink but with the Spirit of the living God, not on tablets of stone but on tablets of human hearts," fathers have the opportunity to leave a legacy in their children's lives. Expressing memories, thoughts, and dreams in writing to our children can be a powerful gift. Writing God's legacy on our children's hearts makes an eternal difference. It can also be helpful and healing for some fatherless fathers to write down their thoughts and emotions about their dads.

On December 31, 1999, and January 1, 2000, I spent time writing down things about my life for my children. The overriding goal was to encourage them in their faith and to let them know the comfort, help, and salvation I had through Jesus Christ. But I continued telling them about my joys and fears about growing up. Included was a list of some of my favorite things and events. There was space for family information. I also noted how I saw God working in their lives—the gifts and talents with which He had blessed them. Memories, thoughts, facts, encourage-ment, trivia, and dreams for my children and grandchildren were included in what could be called a written legacy. Maybe some day it will be helpful to my children or at least a bit interesting, but I've also found it helpful to me. It's good to share our thoughts and feelings, and writing can be a great way to do that.

The following pages of this book are yours for the pur-pose of writing your story. You may find it easier to do it on computer—but be sure to tell someone where to find the disc you put it on! Your story doesn't have to be fancy. You don't have to have a masters' degree in communications. Just write. Have fun with it. Don't sweat it. What you write may be the parental handbook your child needs when he or she becomes a parent. What a gift!

Enjoy! May God bring out His best in you as you serve Him and as you father your children.

Date this was completed: _____

Full name: _____

Parents' names: _____

Born: _____

First home: _____

Current address: _____

Marriage information: _____

_____

Children: _____

My education: _____

_____

Places where I've lived: _____

_____

_____

Jobs I've had: _____

_____

_____

_____

Military experience: _____

Favorites

    Place visited: _____

    Color: _____

    Bible verse: _____

    Book of the Bible: _____

    Movies: _____

    Books: _____

    Vehicle: _____

    Story: _____

    Drink: _____

    Food: _____

    Vegetable: _____

    Fruit: _____

    Television shows: _____

    Restaurant: _____

    Fast-food restaurant: _____

    Sport: _____

    Sports team: _____

    Sport to watch: _____

    Sport to play: _____

    Type of music: _____

    Song: _____

    Card/Board game: _____

    Dessert: _____

States and countries visited: _____

_____

_____

_____

_____

Best friends
    In elementary school: _____
    In high school: _____
    In college: _____
    As an adult: _____
My favorite memories as a child include _____

_____
My least favorite memories as a child include _____

_____
First Car: _____
Date baptized: _____
My first memories/experiences in church include _____

_____
Height and weight when married: _____
Present height and weight: _____
Present shoe size: _____
Nicknames over the years: _____
Musical instruments I played: _____
People who played instrumental roles in my formation as a
man: _____
Information about my parents/grandparents/other family
members: _____

_____
My dreams as a child: _____
My hopes and dreams for you: _____

_____

_____

_____
Things I hope you have learned from me or remember
about me: _____

_____

_____
Regarding your faith in Jesus Christ, I want to say, _____

_____

_____

_____

The advice about parenting I would give you (if God bless-
es you with children): _____

_____

_____

Advice about education: _____

_____

Advice about friendships: _____

_____

Advice about marriage: _____

_____

Advice about finances: _____

_____

Advice about: _____

_____

Other thoughts, events, and people who affected my life: _

_____

_____

_____

_____

_____

_____

_____

_____

_____